Who
Is Jesus?

A Guide to Jesus

Who
Is Jesus?

Stonecroft

Basic Bible Studies
for Everyone

HARVEST HOUSE PUBLISHERS
EUGENE, OREGON

WHO IS JESUS?
Stonecroft Bible Studies
Copyright © 2012 by Stonecroft Ministries, Inc.
www.stonecroft.org
Published by Harvest House Publishers
Eugene, Oregon 97408
www.harvesthousepublishers.com

ISBN 978-0-7369-5187-6 (pbk.)
ISBN 978-0-7369-5188-3 (eBook)

Printed in the United States of America

20 / VP-CD / 10 9 8

Contents

Acknowledgments

Stonecroft wishes to acknowledge Janice Mayo Mathers for her dedication in serving the Lord through Stonecroft. Speaker, author, and National Board Member, Jan is the primary author of revised Stonecroft Bible Studies. We appreciate her love for God's Word and her love for people who need Him. Stonecroft also thanks the team who surrounded Jan in prayer, editing, design, and creative input to make these studies accessible to all.

Welcome to
Stonecroft Bible Studies!

At Stonecroft, we help connect you with God, each other, and your communities.

It doesn't matter where you've been or what you've done... God wants to be in relationship with you. And one place He tells you about Himself is in His Word—the Bible. Whether the Bible is familiar or new to you, its contents will transform your life and bring answers to your biggest questions.

Gather with people in your community—women, men, couples, young and old alike—and explore together what the Bible writers recorded about Jesus. This study will consider why He came, what He said, and what He did, so you can engage with Him in life-transforming ways.

Each chapter of *Who is Jesus?* includes discussion questions to stir up meaningful conversation, specific Scripture verses to investigate, and time for prayer to connect with God and each other.

Discover more of God and His ways through this small-group exploration of the Bible.

Tips for Using This Study

This book has several features that make it easy to use and helpful for your life:

- The page number or numbers given after every Bible reference are keyed to the page numbers in the *Abundant Life Bible.* This handy paperback Bible uses the New Living Translation, a recent version in straightforward, up-to-date language. We encourage you to obtain a copy through your group leader or at stonecroft.org.

- Each chapter ends with a section called "Thoughts, Notes, and Prayer Requests." Use this space for notes or for thoughts that come to you during your group time or study, as well as prayer requests.

- In the back of the book you will find "Journal Pages"—a space available for writing down how the study is changing your life or any other personal thoughts, reactions, and reflections.

- Please make this book and study your own. We encourage you to use it and mark it in any way that helps you grow in your relationship with God!

If you find this study helpful, you may want to investigate other resources from Stonecroft Ministries. Please take a look at "Stonecroft Resources" in the back of the book or online at **stonecroft.org/store.**

stonecroft.org

Introduction

Have you ever wondered why so much attention is paid to Jesus—who He was, what He did, why He did it? Why is it that one man—who lived on this earth less than 40 years, who never traveled farther than 300 miles from the place of His birth—so impacted society that worldwide time is measured by His birth and death? Why is it *His* name that springs to the lips of people when they curse…or when they're desperate?

What is it about Him, that more than 2000 years after He walked this earth, people are still willing to give up their lives for Him or leave the people and places they know in order to tell others about Him? Why do some feel so strongly about Him that they have dedicated their lives to eradicating His impact on society? Can you think of another man who has inspired such strong emotion, such dedication, so many changed lives? And the most provocative question of all—does this man, Jesus, have any relevance to you and me in the twenty-first century?

When people are asked who Jesus is, the answers are as varied as the people questioned.

"He's a historical figure."

"He was the founder of a religion."

"He's no longer relevant, whoever He was."

"He's basically a legend."

"He was a great prophet."

"He was a good man who helped a lot of people."

"We can't really know because He lived so long ago."

"He was a great moral teacher."

"He's the Savior of the world."

"He was a first-century revolutionary and victim of oppression."

"He is the Son of God."

"I don't know."

Who do you say Jesus is?

In this study we are going to take a look at this man who, for more than 2000 years, has continued to evoke such strong reactions. I think you'll find this to be an exciting, even challenging, study as we take a closer look at Jesus and, in the process, a closer look at ourselves.

1

What Does the Bible Say About Jesus?

A young woman stirred and grimaced with unfamiliar pain. Why did her body feel so stiff and bruised? She felt a tiny wriggle beside her, and her eyes shot open in sudden alertness. Her baby!

Ever so quietly, so as not to disturb her husband, she sat up and gathered her tiny son to her breast. Instantly he quieted. She gazed down at him in wonder. Tonight she'd become a mother. This perfect little baby was her son. A wave of love, even exhilaration, swept through her, and she cuddled him more tightly. This night had changed her forever. She would never be the same again. Nothing mattered as much as this child in her arms, and she would do everything in her power to make sure her son had a good life.

Suddenly she froze as shards of remembered truth stabbed through her thoughts. This was no ordinary child. He would not live an ordinary life. She would not be able to keep him from harm. This tiny infant—her son—would also become her Savior.

Prayer

God, as I begin this study about your Son, Jesus, help me to hear for myself and understand that He is indeed the Christ, the Savior of the world (John 4:42b, page 812).

Sources About Jesus

Over time, much has been written about this person known as Jesus. Although the Bible contains the most information about Him, there are numerous other historical sources that refer to Him. Here is what experts say:

> "We have better historical documentation for Jesus than for the founder of any other ancient religion," said Edwin Yamauchi. Sources from outside the Bible corroborate that many people believed Jesus performed healings and was the Messiah, that he was crucified, and that despite this shameful death, his followers, who believed he was still alive, worshiped him as God. One expert documented thirty-nine ancient sources that corroborate more than one hundred facts concerning Jesus' life, teachings, crucifixion, and resurrection. Seven secular sources and several early creeds concern the deity of Jesus, a doctrine "definitely present in the earliest church," according to scholar Gary Habermas.*

Three of the main ancient sources that mention Jesus are from the Roman Empire not long after His time:

- The *Epistles* (letters) of Pliny, a provincial governor in Asia Minor at the time of his writing
- The *Annals* (yearly records of events) by Tacitus, who was a leading lawyer of his day
- *Lives of the Caesars* by Suetonius, who was a scholar and biographer

These writers mentioned both Jesus and His followers. Additionally, Josephus, a Jewish historian born a few years after Jesus' death, recorded facts about Jesus' life and crucifixion in his *Antiquities*.*

---

* Lee Strobel, *The Case for Christ* (Grand Rapids, MI: Zondervan, 1998), page 351.

The Bible, however, is the most exhaustive resource on the life and legacy of Jesus. You may not be familiar with it, and perhaps you aren't sure whether it can be trusted. Much could be said about this question, but briefly, the Bible is by far the most reliable ancient writing we have today. It has been investigated, tested, and trusted by countless people over the centuries. In particular, modern scholarship has helped support its historical trustworthiness.

Just to give you a quick overview, the Bible is divided into two sections—the Old Testament, which has 39 books, and the New Testament, which has 27 books. Jesus is the foundation (or "cornerstone") of both sections.

The Old Testament, besides being a fascinating book of ancient history, contains hundreds of predictions about the birth, life, and death of a man called the Messiah—God's Chosen One. Some of these prophecies are very specific, especially regarding the Messiah's birth and manner of death. And every one of those predictions came true in the life of Jesus precisely as stated in the Old Testament, which was written hundreds to thousands of years before His birth.

Doesn't that make you think that the Bible is more than just another book of ancient history? It is one reason that many people have trusted it as the inspired Word of God, an amazing gift He has given us so we can know Him intimately and have our lives changed by our relationship with Him.

As you read the Bible, test it by asking these questions:

- What is it saying?
- What does it mean?
- What is God saying to me personally?

As you consider these questions, you'll find that the words will begin to have an impact on your life. The Bible will gain more significance for you as you begin to understand how God wants to relate to you and everyone in the world.

What Does the New Testament Say About Jesus?

The New Testament is not only about Jesus' time here on earth before and after His resurrection, but it is also about the people who followed Him both while He was on earth and in the decades following His death and resurrection. The New Testament chronicles what Jesus told us about God, His Father, and His teachings about how we can receive God's life inside us, resulting in a life of compassion, service and fullness, and enjoying life with Him forever after we die.

The first four books of the New Testament, called the *Gospels* (Matthew, Mark, Luke, and John), make up almost half of the New Testament. They are our main source of information about Jesus, and we will be referring to them frequently throughout this study.

As you read through the New Testament, it becomes clear that Jesus is not simply a great religious leader of the world. Neither is He just another great man of the Bible, such as Abraham, Moses, or King David. Remember, every time we write the date and year, we are recognizing the fact that about 2000 years ago Jesus Christ came to earth and split history in two: *BC*—Before Christ, and *AD*—After Christ.* So let's see what this part of the Bible says.

During much of the time Jesus was traveling and teaching publicly, even His disciples, who believed in Him enough to leave their lifestyles and livelihoods to follow Him, were confused about who He really was. They realized He was not just an ordinary man, but they did not know how to reconcile what they were seeing and experiencing with their previously held beliefs. For a vivid example of their confusion, read Mark 4:35-41 (page 764).

Think about this incident for a moment. Imagine being in a boat

---

* *AD* is an abbreviation for Latin words meaning "the year of our Lord." You may also have encountered the terms *CE* and *BCE* ("Common Era" and "Before Common Era"). Since the latter twentieth century, this means of noting the division in time made by Christ's birth has been popularized in academic and scientific publications, and more generally by those who wish to avoid religion or promote sensitivity to non-Christians.

when a terrifying storm hits. You are completely at its mercy—the waves toss your boat about like a piece of driftwood. Imagine the feel of the drenching rain as it chills you, the deafening roar of the wind as the waves crash down around you, and the terror of imminent death.

Now imagine peering through the stormy darkness to see Jesus sleeping peacefully in the midst of the chaos while you are hanging on for dear life. *Is He crazy? Can He truly be so sound asleep? He's not aware of the storm? Impossible!* You shout to Him in panic, and He rouses from His sleep. He looks around and then, as if speaking to an ill-behaved child, He commands the storm, *"Silence! Be still!"*

And just like that, the sea smooths out like glass.

Wouldn't you too wonder, *"Who is this man?"*

How would you have explained what you were seeing?

It was not just His disciples who were grappling with questions about Jesus. Everyone who came in contact with Him had questions. Read Matthew 16:13-16 (page 747).

Put yourself in their position almost 2000 years ago. How would you respond to Jesus' calming of the sea? Who would you have said Jesus was?

Matthew 16 lists some strange explanations, doesn't it? People were so desperate to explain Jesus' unexplainable abilities that they decided

He was the reincarnation of various people who had died: John the Baptist, a relative (some say a cousin) who had been beheaded (Mark 6:14-16, page 766). Elijah, an Old Testament prophet who was taken up into heaven without dying (2 Kings 2:11, page 283). Jeremiah, another Old Testament prophet who had died centuries earlier. Desperate explanations—and every one of them wrong!

People realized that Jesus was not an ordinary man. They knew He was someone special, but they didn't know what to do with Him. And some 2000 years later people still wonder. They still attempt to make Him less than who He was and explain Him away.

Descriptions of Jesus

In the New Testament, we learn much about Jesus. A number of His qualities stand out:

Jesus is eternal. He lived before the beginning of time.

> *He existed before anything else.*
>
> —Colossians 1:17 (page 902)

Jesus existed before He was born as a man. He always has and always will exist. He said,

> *Before Abraham was even born, I Am!*
>
> —John 8:58 (page 818)

I AM was God's name. In Exodus 3:14 (page 45), long before Jesus was born, God identified Himself to Moses as "I Am Who I Am." The Hebrew meaning of the name implies continuous existence.

Jesus claimed equality with God.

> *He called God his Father,*
> *thereby making himself equal with God.*
>
> —John 5:18 (page 813)

Though he was God, he did not think of equality
with God as something to cling to.
Instead, he gave up his divine privileges.

—Philippians 2:6-7 (page 900)

Jesus Himself is the Truth, and His teaching was ultimate truth. He never had to retract or change what He said. He never supposed, guessed, or spoke with uncertainty. A study of His life reveals He had all the attributes of God. He was without sin. He forgave sin. He accepted worship. All these facts and others show us that He is God.

Jesus told him, "I am the way, the truth, and the life.
No one can come to the Father except through me."

—John 14:6 (page 823)

Jesus is unique. His uniqueness is revealed in both His conception and His virgin birth (Luke 1:26-35, pages 779-780). It is revealed in His sinless life and His powerful teachings that showed how God, His Father, sees the world. All this and much more reveal His unparalleled life.

God made Christ, who never sinned,
to be the offering for our sin,
so that we could be made right with God through Christ.

—2 Corinthians 5:21 (page 884)

Jesus is a servant.

Look at my Servant, whom I have chosen.
He is my Beloved, who pleases me.
I will put my Spirit upon him,
and he will proclaim justice to the nations.

—Matthew 12:18 (page 743)

You must have the same attitude that Christ Jesus had.
Though he was God, he did not think of equality with
God as something to cling to. Instead, he gave up his
divine privileges; he took the humble position of a slave
and was born as a human being. When he appeared
in human form, he humbled himself in obedience to
God and died a criminal's death on a cross.

—Philippians 2:5-8 (page 900)

Read Romans 15:8 (page 868) and John 13:3-17 (page 822).

Jesus loves everyone.

The Word became human and made his home among us.
He was full of unfailing love and faithfulness. And we have
seen his glory, the glory of the Father's one and only Son.

—John 1:14 (page 809)

God loved the world so much that he gave his one and
only Son, so that everyone who believes in him will not
perish but have eternal life.

—John 3:16 (page 811)

Jesus is compassionate.

Jesus saw the huge crowd as he stepped from the boat,
and he had compassion on them and healed their sick.

—Matthew 14:14 (page 745)

*Moved with compassion, Jesus reached out and touched
him. "I am willing," he said. "Be healed!"*

—Mark 1:41 (page 762)

Which of these seven descriptions of Jesus has the most significance for you right now? Why?

The Names and Characteristics of Jesus

At the time the Bible was written, names were more deeply connected to the person's identity. They were meant to reveal certain traits
and characteristics about them. Jesus is so great that no one name
could tell us all we need to know about Him. Look up the following
references and note some of the names used to refer to Jesus:

Matthew 1:21 (page 733)

Matthew 1:23 (page 733)

Matthew 3:17 (page 735)

The following passage mentions a name Jesus used of Himself:

> *"I will prove to you that the Son of Man has the authority on earth to forgive sins." Then Jesus turned to the paralyzed man and said, "Stand up, pick up your mat, and go home!"*
>
> —Mark 2:10-11 (page 762)

In Mark 2, Jesus reveals that He is both man (by calling Himself "Son of Man") and God (because He is able to forgive sins). Since only God has the power to forgive sins, this emphasizes Jesus' equality with God. He refers to Himself as the Son of Man and Son of God in other passages as well. Read Matthew 16:16 (page 747).

What name was used of Jesus?

In the next verse (17), Jesus says that God has revealed this name to Simon Peter. To the Jewish mind, *Messiah* meant that Jesus was God's Anointed One and His appointed ruler. *The Son of the living God* meant Jesus was co-eternal and co-equal with God.

What names are used of Jesus in these verses?

Matthew 19:16 (page 750)

Mark 5:6-7 (page 765)

Luke 5:5 (page 784)

These names reveal Jesus' sovereign authority over everything and everyone. Now read John 1:35-36 (page 810).

What title is used here?

This name reveals Jesus as the perfect sacrifice sent to die for the sins of all people. The Bible says in Romans 6:23 (page 861) that the wages of sin is death—separation from God and His life forever. The sacrifice of the lamb in the Old Testament (Leviticus 1:1-5, page 79) symbolized in advance the death of Jesus Christ. God had told the Israelites that He would send the

First Corinthians 1:7 (page 870) uses Jesus' three most common names and titles together as one complete name, the "Lord Jesus Christ." When we call Jesus Christ "Lord," it means we acknowledge that we have put ourselves under His lordship and leadership.

perfect sacrifice to die in the place of sinners. That's why Jesus is called the Lamb of God. See John 3:16 (page 811) and Hebrews 9:13-15 (page 925). Now read the following verses together and note what titles are used of Jesus.

John 1:49 (page 810)

1 Corinthians 1:6-7 (page 870)

As we already read in Matthew 1:23, one of the names for Jesus means "*God is with us.*" We can see that He is God when we read a prophecy of the Messiah's birth in Isaiah 9:6 (page 523). What are His names according to this verse?

Quietly repeat the names of Jesus that you found in the verses. Which name speaks to you the most?

Why?

There are many more names and titles we could review to see Jesus. The disciples called Him Lord because they recognized that He had come from God and deserved their worship and submission. What does He mean to you?

Biblical Prophecies About Jesus

The Bible is an amazingly interconnected book, especially when you realize it was written over a period of about 1500 years by more than 40 different human authors! This supernatural consistency is what you would expect if God is its ultimate Author.

We said earlier in this chapter that Jesus is the foundation of the entire Bible. We can learn about who He is from both the Old Testament and the New Testament, and we can gain confidence in the Bible as we see how Old Testament prophecies about the Messiah, written hundreds of years before Jesus' time, were fulfilled by Him in the New Testament.

Let's take a look at what a few of these prophecies say and how they came true in Jesus.

- Old Testament prophecy that the Messiah would be born

from a virgin: Isaiah 7:14 (page 522) *"The Lord himself will give you the sign. Look! The virgin will conceive a child! She will give birth to a son and will call him Immanuel (which means 'God is with us')."*

New Testament fulfillment by Jesus: Matthew 1:22-23 (page 733) *"All of this occurred to fulfill the Lord's message through his prophet: 'Look! The virgin will conceive a child! She will give birth to a son, and they will call him Immanuel, which means "God is with us."'"*

- Old Testament prophecy regarding the Messiah's place of birth: Micah 5:2 (page 706) *"You, O Bethlehem Ephrathah, are only a small village among all the people of Judah. Yet a ruler of Israel will come from you, one whose origins are from the distant past."*

   New Testament fulfillment by Jesus: Matthew 2:1a (page 734) *"Jesus was born in Bethlehem in Judea, during the reign of King Herod."*

- Old Testament prophecy that the Messiah would be rejected by His own people: Isaiah 53:3 (page 559) *"He was despised and rejected—a man of sorrows, acquainted with deepest grief. We turned our backs on him and looked the other way. He was despised, and we did not care."*

   New Testament fulfillment by Jesus: John 1:11 (page 809) *"He came to his own people, and even they rejected him."*

- Old Testament prophecy that the Messiah would be betrayed by a friend: Psalm 41:9 (page 432) *"Even my best friend, the one I trusted completely, the one who shared my food, has turned against me."*

   New Testament fulfillment by Jesus: Mark 14:10 (page 775) *"Judas Iscariot, one of the twelve disciples, went to the leading priests to arrange to betray Jesus to them."*

- Old Testament prophecy that the Messiah would be resurrected from the dead: Psalm 16:10 (page 420) *"For you will not leave my soul among the dead or allow your holy one to rot in the grave."*

New Testament fulfillment by Jesus: Matthew 28:5-6 (page 760) *"The angel spoke to the women. 'Don't be afraid!' he said. 'I know you are looking for Jesus, who was crucified. He isn't here! He is risen from the dead, just as he said would happen. Come, see where his body was lying.'"*

What thoughts or questions do you have as you consider these Old Testament prophecies and New Testament fulfillments concerning Jesus?

Both the Old and New Testaments have much more to tell us about who Jesus is, and we will explore some of those things in the rest of this book.

What do you now think about Jesus? Are you willing to trust what the Bible says about Him? Could anyone but God have sent Him? Let's end with one of the most overwhelming descriptions of all, which is found in Colossians 1:15-20 (page 902). List how this passage describes Jesus.

Perhaps the most profound statement in this passage is the first one:

Christ is the visible image of the invisible God.

—Colossians 1:15a

Think of that! Jesus is the *visible* image of the invisible God! When we read about Jesus' words and actions, His attitudes and behaviors, as He walked this earth, *we are seeing a picture of God Himself, the Maker of the Universe.* We are seeing His heart, feeling the power and safety of His love!

What an incredible gift God gave us in the Bible. Through those inspired words, Jesus (God) becomes visible to us, as we learn all we can about this man by whom all time is measured!

––––––––– *Personal Reflection and Application* –––––––––

From this chapter,

I see…

I believe…

I will…

Prayer

Father God, thank you that every word of yours is true and that your Word took on human form in Jesus. Thank you for your unfailing love and faithfulness as I learn about your Son (Proverbs 30:5, page 503, and John 1:14, page 809).

--- *Thoughts, Notes, and Prayer Requests* ---

What Did Jesus Say?

One of my favorite stories from Jesus' life is found in John 9 (pages 818-819). In this chapter, He heals a man who has been blind since birth. A huge uproar ensues. The religious leaders, desperate for an explanation for what they've just witnessed, pummel the poor man with questions. *Who healed you? Why did he do it? How did he do it?*

Though the man answers every question the best he can, they are not satisfied. They repeat the same questions over and over, as if they are deaf to his responses. Finally you can almost see him throw his hands up in frustration. He says, *"But I know this: I was blind, and now I can see!"*

I feel sorry for the religious leaders. They were the ones who were supposed to have all the spiritual answers, but here is this man named Jesus—a lowly carpenter from nowhere important—getting people all stirred up with His talk about being the Son of God. His miracles couldn't be explained away. Here's this other man the whole town knows was born blind, suddenly claiming he can see! *No wonder they don't like his answers.* Just like the disciples who saw Jesus stop the storm, the answers did not fit with what they had always known to be true about nature: People don't just speak storms away; blind men don't just suddenly start seeing.

Prayer

Father, thank you that Jesus' words and all of Scripture give me the wisdom to receive the salvation that comes by trusting in Him. I understand that all Scripture is inspired by you; and it is all useful to teach me what is true and to make me realize what is wrong in my life. Thank you that it corrects me when I am wrong, teaches me to do what is right, and equips me to do every good work (2 Timothy 3:15-17, page 915).

It is very disconcerting to be faced with irrefutable proof of something you would have never, in your wildest dreams, believed to be true. But facts are facts. A blind man who can suddenly count how many fingers you are holding up in front of him is hard to argue with.

How do you think the religious leaders felt when they could not explain how the blind man was healed?

How do you think the blind man felt when the religious leaders did not believe his testimony?

Can you remember a time when you were given proof of something you had been sure was not the truth? How did it affect you?

Jesus' Claims About Himself

But it wasn't just Jesus' miracles that threw all the religious leaders into a frenzy. It was also some of the outrageous claims He was making about Himself. Let's take a look at some of those statements.

One of the names Jesus used for Himself was "I AM." You might remember that we mentioned this name in the last chapter. I AM is the name of God and conveys the meaning that He always is, always was, and always will be. It emphasizes continued existence and completeness. Jesus refers to the fact of His continued existence when speaking to some people in John 8:56-59 (page 818): *"Your father Abraham rejoiced as he looked forward to my coming. He saw it and was glad."*

This outraged His listeners. *"You aren't even fifty years old,"* they said. *"How can you say you have seen Abraham?"*

Jesus' answer only angered them even more. *"I tell you the truth, before Abraham was even born, I AM!"*

Blasphemy was a serious offense in Jesus' time (punishable by death), and for any human to claim to be God was serious blasphemy. So you can understand their outrage. They were protecting what they held dear; and it was easier to hold on to what they had always believed than to dare trust the unexplainable, miraculous things happening before their very eyes.

And this is not the only time Jesus referred to Himself as I AM. God first introduced Himself as I AM when commissioning Moses to be the leader of the Israelites (Exodus 3:14, page 45). Throughout the Gospels, Jesus continued to call Himself I AM. He completed what seemed to be incomplete sentences (I AM...) with words describing all He is to those who trust Him. Read the following Bible verses and finish the I AM statements Jesus made:

John 13:19 (page 822). I am...

John 8:12 (page 817). I am…

John 10:9 (page 819). I am…

John 10:11 (page 819). I am…

John 10:36 (page 819). I am…

John 11:25 (page 820). I am…

John 6:48 (page 815). I am…

John 14:6 (page 823). I am...

Isn't the verse in John 14 astounding? Jesus is the *way* to God. He is the *truth* of God and about God. He is the very *life* of God in those who receive Him. In Jesus, *everything is covered*! No matter what we are facing at any given time, there is an I AM statement from Jesus, a specific characteristic of God in Jesus. What characteristic do you most identify with right now and why?

Jesus Has the Authority to Speak for God

If you met someone who said He was from God and then backed up His claim with fulfilled prophecy and by doing miracles, wouldn't you listen very carefully to Him? The people did listen, although they did not always respond in belief. Read Matthew 7:28-29 (page 738), which comes right after Jesus gave the teaching known as the Sermon on the Mount.

What was the reaction of the crowds?

Why did they respond in the way they did?

Whether or not His listeners believed that Jesus' authority to teach and perform miracles came from God the Father, Jesus made it clear. One time Jesus broke the Jewish rules by healing a man on the Sabbath. When the leaders harassed Him for this, He responded:

> I tell you the truth, the Son can do nothing by himself. He does only what he sees the Father doing. Whatever the Father does, the Son also does. For the Father loves the Son and shows him everything he is doing. In fact, the Father will show him how to do even greater works than healing this man. Then you will truly be astonished. For just as the Father gives life to those he raises from the dead, so the Son gives life to anyone he wants.
>
> I tell you the truth, those who listen to my message and believe in God who sent me have eternal life. They will never be condemned for their sins, but they have already passed from death into life (John 5:19-21,24, page 813).

Could it be any clearer? Jesus had God's authority to heal and do other miracles. He spoke the Father's message, and anyone who listened to and believed Him was given life forever—the same kind of life God has.

Jesus taught God's message in three ways: sermons, parables, and prophecies. We're going to look at all three, but let's start with His sermons. A *sermon* is a speech that gives moral and religious instruction. Jesus preached many amazing sermons, and their message was life-changing for any who would believe and put His teaching into practice. We're only going to look at one here, but it is perhaps His most famous.

A Sermon Jesus Gave

The Sermon on the Mount is partially recounted in both the Gospels of Luke and Mark, but Matthew, who was one of Jesus' disciples, recorded it in detail. It's possible that Jesus taught these things, or parts of them, many times as He traveled around the country.

You can read this famous teaching in Matthew 5:1–7:29 (pages 735-738). Let's read it by sections and note what you see to be the main thought in each one.

Matthew 5:1-12 (pages 735-736)

Matthew 5:13-16 (page 736)

Matthew 5:17-20 (page 736)

Matthew 5:21-26 (page 736)

Matthew 5:27-30 (page 736)

Matthew 5:31-32 (page 736)

Matthew 5:33-37 (page 736)

Matthew 5:38-42 (page 737)

Matthew 5:43-48 (page 737)

Matthew 6:1-15 (page 737)

Matthew 6:24-34 (pages 737-738)

Matthew 7:1-12 (page 738)

Matthew 7:13-20 (page 738)

Matthew 7:21-27 (page 738)

What parts of Jesus' teaching from this sermon surprise you?

Do some of the things Jesus is teaching seem impossible? Why do you think He would say them?

Consider the *who* and *when* of the Sermon on the Mount. Jesus was speaking to a Jewish audience, with perhaps a few curious Roman soldiers and others thrown in. The time was toward the beginning or middle of His travels, before He *"was handed over to die because of our sins, and...raised to life to make us right with God"* (Romans 4:25, page 860). Isn't it wonderful that the Father provided Jesus for us? We could never meet God's standards without Him!

What does Jesus reveal to you about His Father, and why?

Which topics in the sermon did you find most relevant to your life right now?

A wonderful aspect of studying the Bible is that its relevance never diminishes. Different parts speak to us in different ways, depending on what we're experiencing at the time. The Sermon on the Mount is an example of this.

Parables Jesus Told

Now let's take a look at the second way Jesus taught, which is through parables. A *parable* is a short, simple story that communicates a spiritual truth. Jesus told many different parables that are recorded in the Gospels. He drew illustrations from nature or from familiar, everyday happenings to explain a moral or spiritual truth that was less familiar. One of the benefits of using parables in teaching is to present powerful truth in an interesting and memorable way, but in a way that does not immediately overwhelm the listeners.

Another aspect of parables as Jesus used them is that they often had a hidden meaning that needed further explanation. He used this method when He wanted to conceal the meaning from His enemies. That way, those who were trying to trap Him could find no direct statements to use against Him.

The Bible tells us that not everyone can understand what Jesus said. For example, read 1 Corinthians 2:13-16 (page 871). How are we able to understand Jesus' parables?

Isn't it incredible to think that when we have God's Spirit working within us, we can *know* the wonderful things God has for us. He gives us the mind of Christ! And because of that, we have understanding.

However, without God's Spirit, Jesus' words can seem like nonsense. His enemies were often incensed by His parables because they couldn't understand what He meant. It sounded like foolishness to them, but it still raised their suspicions. They desperately wanted to catch Him saying something they could use against Him, but parables made it difficult.

The "Parable of the Farmer Scattering Seed" is one of Jesus' best-known parables. (It is also known as the "Parable of the Sower.") Matthew, Mark, and Luke each record Jesus' explanation of this parable, but let's just look at Luke's version. First read Luke 8:4-8 (page 788).

Now read Jesus' explanation of the parable in Luke 8:11-15 (pages 788-789).

What does the parable say the seed represents?

List the things that prevent the seed of God's Word from taking root in people's lives (verses 12-13).

The seed mentioned in verse 14 takes root, but it never grows properly. What prevents this from happening?

According to verse 15, why does some seed yield more than others?

Now apply this parable to your own life. What is currently the biggest obstacle to God's Word taking root and producing fruit in your heart?

Depending on what you think your obstacle is, what changes can you make to allow God's Word into your life so it takes root, or allow it to grow and flourish?

It's no wonder parables are such an effective way to teach. First, they tell a story—and everyone loves a story. Couldn't you visualize the seed being stepped on or the birds flocking toward an unexpected feast?

Second, they paint a picture we can easily relate to. When you read the explanation about the thorns choking out the seed, for instance, couldn't you draw a comparison to all the worries and busyness that can keep you from flourishing in God's love and in your understanding of the Bible? Analogies always help us see a situation more clearly—it's why Jesus used them.

The most famous parable Jesus ever spoke is the next one we'll consider. Though it was told to a Jewish audience, it speaks to the heart of nearly everyone. Can you guess which one it is?

The "Parable of the Lost Son"—traditionally, the "Prodigal Son"—is recorded only in Luke's Gospel. Read Luke 15:11-32 (page 798).

What, or who, is Jesus' focus in this parable? Why do you think that?

The traditional name for Jesus' most well-known story—the "Parable of the Prodigal Son" focuses on the son's actions and character. (The word *prodigal* means "recklessly spendthrift," according to Webster.) The newer name—the "Parable of the Lost Son"—focuses on the son's condition and need. It also better reflects the theme of Jesus' previous stories in Luke 15 (pages 797-798): the "Parable of the Lost Sheep" and the "Parable of the Lost Coin."

In verses 20-24, does the father accept the son's apology? How does he respond to his son's return?

There is one discontented person in the story. When the older son complains, what does the father say had to be done (verse 32)?

Can you see why this parable has always upset people who think they have done everything God wants? It must have enraged the Jewish leaders.

Who do you think Jesus wants us to copy: the older son, who believes he has always obeyed his father but is resentful toward him; or the younger son, who has disobeyed terribly but realizes his need and returns to his father?

Jesus is always revealing God the Father—how He thinks and feels and what He does.

What do you think Jesus is trying to reveal about the Father in this parable?

More examples. If you would like to consider more examples of parables, Matthew 13 (pages 744-745) is an interesting chapter. It's another sermon Jesus preached, but there are seven different parables woven into it. Take a few minutes to read through it if you have time, and note the subject matter of each parable:

1. Matthew 13:1-23

2. Matthew 13:24-30,36-43

3. Matthew 13:31-32

4. Matthew 13:33-35

5. Matthew 13:44

6. Matthew 13:45-46

7. Matthew 13:47-50

Now let's take a look at the third method Jesus used to teach: prophecies.

Prophecies by Jesus

A *prophecy* comes from speaking under the influence of God's guidance. Earlier, we read some of the prophecies the Old Testament prophets gave concerning the coming of the Messiah and how those prophecies were fulfilled in Jesus.

Jesus also gave many prophecies. He prophesied about His betrayal, His death, His resurrection, and His ascension. He predicted Peter's denial, that He would be forsaken by His disciples, and that He would meet His disciples in Galilee after His death and resurrection. He also predicted that after He left earth, He would one day return.

Let's look at some of these New Testament prophecies. Beside each reference, list the prophecy.

Mark 14:71-72 (page 776)

Luke 24:5-7 (page 807)

John 5:25-29 (page 813)

John 12:32-33 (page 822)

Jesus often prophesied about the last days. Turn to Matthew 24:1-3 (page 754). What two questions did the disciples ask Jesus?

1.

2.

The temple prophecy (verse 2) was fulfilled in AD 70—about 37 years after Jesus' death—when the Romans completely destroyed Jerusalem and the temple buildings.

Jesus answered His disciples' second question in Matthew 24:36-39 (page 755).

What did He tell them?

In spite of Jesus' answer, ever since, people have still tried to pin-point this date. Some have gone so far as to sell all of their belongings and head for the hills to await the date they think is predicted. While on earth, Jesus made it clear. *No one* but God the Father knew.

The main thing to remember is this—when we know Jesus as our Savior, we can trust Him with our future. His promises to us are just as true now as they have been throughout the ages. Here are some of my favorites:

- Hebrews 13:5b (page 928) *"I will never fail you. I will never abandon you."*

- Philippians 4:6-7 (page 901) *"Don't worry about anything; instead, pray about everything. Tell God what you need, and thank him for all he has done. Then you will experience God's peace, which exceeds anything we can understand. His peace will guard your hearts and minds as you live in Christ Jesus."*

- Philippians 4:19 (page 901) *"This same God who takes care of me will supply all your needs from his glorious riches, which have been given to us in Christ Jesus."*

Do you have a favorite promise you rely on?

When your heart begins to feel anxious, reflect on God and His wonderful promises. He will infuse you with confidence in Him and strengthen your trust in Him; He will help you endure the trials, hardships, and discouragements that are part of life; He will motivate you to live with courage. He will never leave you alone, so you have nothing to be afraid of!

Jesus' Words to Us

Before we close this section on "What Did Jesus Say?" remember what we considered earlier. Jesus said that His message—*all* of His teaching, *all* of His parables, and *all* of His prophecies—was from His Father. That's how we can be assured His words are truth—all He said and did came from God, His Father.

Even Jesus' enemies, the guards working for the leading priests and Pharisees, were impressed with what He said. What did they say in John 7:45-46 (page 816)?

God has often used people to voice His words. All through the Old Testament we read of times when God spoke to different prophets, priests, and kings. The Bible notes this by using phrases like "God said…" or "the Lord said…" or "the Word of the Lord came to…" God also spoke to people in the New Testament. Look up the following references to see who some of these people were, and note it after each verse:

Mark 1:10-11 (page 761)

John 1:32-33 (page 809)

Acts 11:4-9 (page 840)

God also spoke in other ways to people. How did He speak to Cornelius in Acts 10:3-6 (page 839)?

Another time, the leaders of the church in Antioch were worshiping the Lord and fasting when He spoke to them. Read Acts 13:2-3 (page 841). What means did God use here?

God speaks to us today also. How does Hebrews 1:1-2a (page 920) say He does this?

Where do we find the words of His Son, Jesus?

Yes—in the Bible. Every time we read the Bible, God is speaking to our minds and hearts. Isn't that wonderful to think about? Our responsibility is to listen to, believe, and obey what we are reading.

Now read 1 Thessalonians 2:13 (page 905).

Notice the last phrase: *"And this word continues to work in you who believe."* How incredible to know that God's message never stops having its effect, and that His Word is still working in us today.

Think of it—we can read God's thoughts when we read His Word. Again, what a gift the Bible is—God's inspired, written Word!

Take a few minutes to contemplate what you have learned about Jesus so far and some of the things He has spoken to you. Write out your thoughts.

 *Personal Reflection and Application*

From this chapter,

I see…

I believe…

I will…

Prayer

Thank you, Father, that your Word remains forever! Thank you that your Word is the truth that frees me (1 Peter 1:25, page 934, and John 8:32, page 817).

———— *Thoughts, Notes, and Prayer Requests* ————

What Did Jesus Do?

Jesus often came into people's lives in unexpected ways, as He did with this woman...

If ever a life was out of control, it was hers. She hadn't planned for things to turn out this way. It's not like she grew up thinking, *Someday I want to be married five times. Someday I want to be the joke of the town. I want women to whisper behind my back and men to sneer.* But that's exactly how her life did turn out. That's why she came to the town well at the hottest part of the day when everyone else was resting—she didn't want to encounter anyone.

At the sound of a skittering rock, she whirled around to see a man standing nearby. A Jew! It was obvious from His appearance. What was a Jew doing here? She steeled herself against the gaze of contempt she was certain was being directed at her.

To her complete shock, though, He spoke to her. Odder yet, all He asked her for was a drink of water. She shaded her eyes for a better look. This didn't make any sense at all. The Jews hated the Samaritans. They refused to even speak to them. Something was different about this man. What could He want?

Half curious, half fearful, the woman held out a pitcher of water. She had no inkling her life was about to change forever, that the shame of her past would be wiped out, and through her encounter with this man, she would be the catalyst to bring new life to her entire village (John 4:1-42, pages 811-812).

⮘⮘

Prayer

Lord, you've said that if I belong to Christ, I am a new person. My old life is gone, and a new one has begun. Help me as I learn about this and other amazing things you have done for me (2 Corinthians 5:17, page 884).

Before we go further in looking at what Jesus did, let's consider an important question about the four books of the Bible from which we get most of our information about Him. This will help us appreciate the lengths to which God went in giving the world the message of His Son, Jesus.

Why *Four* Gospels?

We have been using the Gospels of Matthew, Mark, Luke, and John as our main source material on the life of Jesus. Have you noticed that each of the writers seems to have a different emphasis? This is because each writer had a different background and experience. Each of them was also writing to a different group of people, and for a different purpose.

None of the four writers attempted to write a historical or chronological biography of Jesus' entire time on earth. Inspired by the Holy Spirit, each selected material from Jesus' life and teaching that emphasized the particular portrait of Jesus they desired to present to a specific audience.

All these individual characteristics were coordinated by the Holy Spirit as He inspired the writing. Taken together, the four Gospels give us a good picture of what Jesus said and did during His life on earth.

- *Mark* was the first of the four Gospel writers to write about Jesus. His target audience was the citizens of Rome, so they could have a record of the words and deeds of Jesus. Mark had worked with Paul and Barnabas, the first missionary team to take the Gospel to the Roman world. Later, he worked with Peter, one of Jesus' disciples. It was from Peter that Mark learned many of the details of Jesus' teaching and activities. His biography of Jesus (The Gospel of Mark) emphasizes the work of Christ as the perfect Servant of God.

- *Matthew* had traveled with Jesus for three years and was part of the twelve men Jesus selected to be His closest disciples. He wrote to reveal to the Jews that Jesus was the promised Messiah for whom they were looking. The Jews needed to see how Jesus fulfilled the Old Testament prophecies of their coming King. In his Gospel, Matthew told them how the nation rejected Jesus and His kingdom. Matthew's book is especially meaningful to those who are familiar with the Old Testament.

- Gentiles (all non-Jews) also needed to hear about Jesus, so Luke's target audience was the Greeks. *Luke* was a Greek doctor who had traveled with Paul. His Gospel is the most detailed record we have of Jesus' life. He conducted careful historical research, studied the writings of the apostles, and interviewed eyewitnesses.

   What he wrote about the conception and birth of Christ must have been learned from Mary herself. We believe this because the things he wrote about her were not public knowledge. For example, Luke wrote about her actual thoughts concerning what she experienced. (See Luke 1:29,34, page 779; Luke 2:19,51, pages 781-782.)

- Finally, *John*, another one of the disciples who had traveled with Jesus for three years, emphasized the fact that

Jesus was the Son of God. In the beginning of his Gospel, John presents the pre-existence of Christ and the fact that He is the Creator of all things. He explains that the Son is a distinct personality from the Father. He also clearly states that Jesus is one with God.

What impact does knowing the authors' backgrounds have on your ability to believe these primary sources on Jesus?

Before looking at how God's Son spent His time on earth, let's fill in a little more background. It's crucial to realize that Jesus had already existed forever. There are four specific and important verses in the Gospel of John that confirm the fact that Jesus is the Creator. These verses present His uniqueness, His oneness with God, His incarnation (His taking on a human body), and His Sonship. Read John 1:1-3,14 (page 809).

When John refers to "*the Word*," he means Jesus. That is why "Word" is capitalized. Isn't this amazing? The one who had existed as God from eternity past came to earth to be *Immanuel*—"God with us"!

How old was Jesus when He began His public teaching and traveling (Luke 3:23, page 782)?

Who commissioned His work (1 John 4:9, page 943)?

What did Jesus say His Heavenly Father is always doing (John 5:17-20, page 813)?

What, or who, was the source and center of Jesus' work?

What insight do you gain from these verses about Jesus?

Don't you think it's wonderful that we can have the life of Jesus in us and share His relationship with the Father? Only God could think of such a plan!

What Jesus Did

Let's look at some of the things Jesus did with His time. Write your findings next to the references.

John 4:7-10 (pages 811-812)

Mark 1:21 (page 761)

Mark 1:32-34 (pages 761-762)

Mark 1:35 (page 762)

Mark 1:38 (page 762)

Mark 6:7-12 (page 766)

Mark 10:13-16 (pages 770-771)

Imagine you were alive during these times. Which of the experiences would you most have wanted to observe or participate in? Why?

The verses we've just read don't even scratch the surface of all Jesus did while on earth. Read the very last words John wrote in his book to see what he says about this (John 21:25, page 829).

"The whole world could not contain the books..." His life was cut short, His time limited, but not a minute was wasted. He saw the great need of the people around Him, and He was tireless in His response. He revealed the Father to those around Him and gave them His Father's message (John 17:4-8, page 825). He saw their desperate need for a relationship with God, and He showed the full extent of His love by dying and rising again to bring them back to God.

Jesus Performed Miracles

One of the things Jesus is most noted for is performing miracles. Word of these miracles spread quickly. Wherever He went, people flocked around, desperate for healing or to have some other need met. Altogether, the Gospels report 34 miracles, but there were far more than that.

A close look at the miracles Jesus performed shows His God-given authority over all things. Read about the following miracles, and note what Jesus had authority over:

Luke 4:33-36 (page 784)

Luke 5:4-10 (pages 784-785)

Mark 1:40-42 (page 762)

Luke 7:11-17 (page 787)

Awesome, isn't it? There is nothing Jesus doesn't have authority over! His power is greater than any other power, and nothing at all can ever stop Him! But there were reasons why Jesus revealed what our all-powerful God could do. Read John 20:30-31 (pages 828-829).

What was one of Jesus' purposes in performing miraculous signs?

God is so merciful to us. He didn't send His Son just to overawe us with displays of power, but so that we could have life—His kind of life!

Jesus Showed Compassion

We just read of some amazing miracles that clearly revealed Jesus' power, authority, and purpose. We don't have to look much further to see another purpose for these supernatural acts. Through them, and in all He does, we see His overflowing compassion—compassion that moved, perhaps compelled, Him to action.

In the following passages, what actions did Jesus take as a result of His compassion?

Matthew 14:14 (page 745)

Mark 1:41 (page 762)

Mark 6:34 (page 766)

John 4:7-10 (pages 811-812)

Luke 18:15-16 (page 800)

Compassion leads to action. The compassion of Christ led Him to heal the brokenhearted, heal the physical bodies of many, and teach those willing to learn. The compassion of Christ led Him to go out of His way to be with people who were marginalized, devalued, or simply never noticed. Jesus noticed people, and His love for women, men, boys, and girls drew Him to respond to their needs, their deepest needs—their greatest need.

What does Jesus' compassion tell you about God, His Father?

What action did God the Father do that revealed His heart of compassion?

He could have done nothing greater than send His own Son, Jesus, to live among us and die for us.

How has compassion motivated you to action?

In what areas or with what group of people do you want to show more Christlike compassion?

Jesus Was a Servant

Jesus' entire life teaches us to serve. In John 13, nearing the end of His time on earth, Jesus shares with His disciples the importance of serving one another. Read the following passages, and note what stands out to you about how Jesus communicated the necessity of service.

John 13:1-15 (page 822)

What does the second part of verse 1 tell you about His motivation?

Mark 9:33-35 (page 770)

Jesus' words were directly connected with His actions. As with any character quality or attitude that is valued, words alone will never suffice. Jesus' attitude of service was modeled throughout His life. It sprang from His heart, and it was seen and acknowledged by those around Him. Read the following verses:

Matthew 20:28 (page 751)

Philippians 2:5-8 (page 900)

Mark 10:43-44 (page 771)

We see this non-negotiable message of service taught, lived, and embodied by Christ throughout His earthly life and after His resurrection. Jesus' entire life was a life of service, often in very down-to-earth ways.

Read John 21:1-13 (page 829).

In His resurrected body, Jesus continued to reveal the heart and will of His Father by serving His disciples. And His life of service was lived out and taught by them through the presence of the Holy Spirit. Read 1 Peter 5:2-4 (page 937).

> What challenge does Peter give to those in leadership with regard to service?

After years of walking with His disciples, after years of their questions, doubts, fears, even betrayal, Jesus continued to serve them. This is not just another personality trait or characteristic. God is love (1 John 4:8-10, page 943). Jesus is God, and His love was communicated in all the ways He served. It was not dependent on how people treated Him. He loved, and He served. And, Jesus has called us to belong to Him and live out His life. Isn't it natural that service is an indispensable component of our following Him?

Although we are Jesus' servants, our connection with Him is still all about relationship. On the night before His death, Jesus said, *"I no longer call you slaves, because a master doesn't confide in his slaves. Now you are my friends, since I have told you everything the Father told me"* (John 15:15, page 824).

Every day we are called to love and serve those around us. Read 1 John 4:11-12 (page 943). Who has God called you to serve?

Jesus Did His Father's Will

Loving, serving, and doing God's will cannot be separated. Jesus' life showed this. Sometimes it's easy to think of God's will as something separate. But take a more careful look at Jesus. He was sharing the life of His Father with everyone around Him who would receive it. He was connecting people—those who were willing—with His all-loving and all-giving Father. Read John 6:38 (page 814).

If you look at only this verse, can it seem as though Jesus is saying something like, "I just follow God's orders"?

But let's take a look at the surrounding verses now (John 6:35-37, 39-40, page 814). For each verse, write what is connected with Jesus' doing the will of God.

Verse 35

Verse 36

Verse 37

Verse 39

Verse 40

Overall, how would you summarize what Jesus is doing as He carries out His Father's will? How does it relate to you and every person alive today?

Aren't you glad that Jesus came to do God's will? Doesn't it make you eager to also do His will and share His life with others?

God is doing everything to ensure our success in following His will. What does Philippians 2:12b-13 (page 900) say about this?

Isn't this amazing? God obviously understands our weaknesses, so

He gives us both the *desire* and the *power* to do His will. We are not in this alone. God empowers us to live in a way that attracts others to Him. We are called to know Jesus and to make Him known. God wants us to fulfill our purpose, even as Jesus fulfilled His purpose.

> He tells us how to do this in Romans 12:2 (page 866). What does this verse say to you?

Isn't that interesting? Transformation comes by way of changed thinking. Allow God to change the way you think and it will change the way you behave. That's why God sent His Son to live on this earth as a man. Through Jesus' words and actions, He challenges the way people think and offers a new way. God wants us to experience the exhilaration that comes through knowing His will for us, which is good and pleasing and perfect. This is a life beyond anything we ever dreamed possible!

> As Jesus' time on earth was nearing its fulfillment (in fact, it was His last day with His disciples before His death), He gathered them together. Among His final words was one very significant command. Read John 13:34-35 (page 823). What was His command?

Love is what matters. God's love in us is what gives our work, our service, our play, our very lives the significance and meaning we long for.

Take a few minutes right now to think about what this means to you. If you were to allow God's love to flow through you to others, it would change your behavior at home, at work, everywhere, wouldn't it?

How would it change your behavior? Take your time and be specific.

It is our loving, serving, and compassionate behavior toward everyone around us that will reveal Jesus in and through us. All He said and did revealed God's love, who He is, and what He's like. That is *our* work, as well. No matter what we are doing, as we live life closely connected to Jesus, we will reveal God's love to those around us.

──────── *Personal Reflection and Application* ────────

From this chapter,

I see...

I believe...

I will...

Prayer

God, since you love me so much, I surely ought to love others. If I do that, people will see that you live in me, and your love will be brought to full expression (1 John 4:11-12, page 943).

Thoughts, Notes, and Prayer Requests

4

Why Did Jesus Come?

Prayer

God, it overwhelms me to think that you did not spare your own Son, but gave Him up for me. And you will also give me everything else I need. Open my heart and mind to what you want me to know through this study (Romans 8:32, page 863).

One of the most amazing things about the Bible is that it shows us what God thinks about things! Every time we read it we discover more about Him. In the process, His thoughts and His ways penetrate deeply into our thinking and behavior. The result is changed thinking and actions—transformation! *"Who can know the LORD's thoughts? Who knows enough to teach him?' But we understand these things, for we have the mind of Christ"* (1 Corinthians 2:16, page 871).

So far, what from this study has challenged the way you think?

Share.

Before we talk about why Jesus came, let's quickly recap what we've already studied. We've learned Jesus has various names that describe both who He is and what He does. If you recall, several of His names show us that He and God are one. Two we looked at in particular were in Isaiah 9:6 (page 523). What are they?

1.

2.

We've learned that Jesus used three different methods of teaching. Can you list those? (See page 35 of this book.)

1.

2.

3.

Using these methods, Jesus taught us what God is like. We see that Jesus continuously reached out in compassion to hurting people, healing them and meeting their needs. His miracles were life-changing; everywhere He went lives were transformed.

Jesus' Ultimate Purpose

Now let's look at why Jesus came. As God's Son, what was His ultimate purpose in leaving the splendor and perfection of heaven to come to an imperfect and fallen earth? Jesus was fully man, and He remained fully God. Why would He voluntarily conceal His glory and take on human form and limitations? Let's look at the following passages to see what the Bible says about this:

John 1:17-18 (page 809)

John 3:16-17 (page 811)

Matthew 20:28 (page 751)

This is just a small sampling of many places that reveal the same reasons for Jesus coming to earth. How would you summarize these passages?

But why do we need to be saved, as John 3:17 says? Why do we need to be ransomed, as Matthew 20:28 says? The Bible tells us that God's desire has always been to have close relationship with us, His creation. True relationship is not forced. It is entered into willingly by both parties. When God created us, He gifted us with a free will—the ability to choose for ourselves. He did this knowing that His creation would reject Him. And that is exactly what happened.

The first to reject Him was a beautiful, powerful angel who is sometimes called Lucifer. In his pride, he wanted to take God's place. Read Isaiah 14:12-14 (page 528).

After this angel sinned against God, he became the creature we now call Satan. He tempted Adam and Eve to disobey their Creator. Eve was deceived by Satan and sinned (2 Corinthians 11:3, page 887), and Adam chose to disobey (Romans 5:12, page 860).

What difference do you see between Eve's decision and Adam's?

It's interesting to contemplate, isn't it, but the end result was the same. Both suffered the terrible consequence of separation from God—often called spiritual death—as a result of misusing their gift of free will—sinning, in other words. Since that time, every human being has been born without the life and presence of God in their lives. And as a result, every human being has misused the gift of free will to try to live independently of God. Every human being has sinned. Romans 3:23 (page 859) says,

> *Everyone has sinned; we all fall*
> *short of God's glorious standard.*

Sin is any attitude or behavior that does not meet God's standard. It's indifference or opposition to God. It's the natural, inevitable result of a broken relationship with Him. This broken relationship interrupted the wonderful life God intended for us, His creation. Until Adam and Eve chose to disobey God's one restriction, they had lived a life of harmony in the beautiful Garden of Eden. Every day, in the cool of the evening, God walked with them through the garden. Imagine the sweet, intimate friendship they must have enjoyed during those evening strolls at the most beautiful time of day. Their work was done, and they could relax and enjoy the beauty with which God had surrounded them.

But then they made that devastating, self-centered choice that destroyed the life they'd enjoyed up to that moment. Their relationship with God was cut off as an unfamiliar shame sprang up between them. Instead of meeting Him at the end of their day, as they'd always done, they hid from Him. And human beings have been hiding from God ever since.

Their separation from God brought both spiritual and physical death. The lush, beautiful garden could no longer be their home. Now their work became laborious and tedious as they struggled to sustain themselves. Sickness and pain, heartache and despair, anger and frustration became familiar companions. Worst of all, the evening strolls with their Creator were lost forever.

But God did not stop loving His creation. He still desired a relationship with people in spite of their sin. He had us in His heart. Romans 6:23 (page 861) says,

> *The wages of sin is death,*
> *but the free gift of God is eternal life*
> *through Christ Jesus our Lord.*

There is only one way to receive God's gift. According to John 3:16-17 (page 811), what is it?

In other words, there is absolutely nothing any human being can do on their own to remove the stain of sin and regain God's life—eternal life. We can work our fingers to the bone doing every good thing we can think of, but it will not remove the separation between us and God. Until we acknowledge Jesus—whom God sent—and the price He paid for us, we will get nowhere.

Jesus Is Our Substitute

Throughout the Old Testament, God decreed that the death of an innocent, sinless substitute (such as a lamb) could cover, or make amends for, the sin of a person, so they would not be punished for it. But until Jesus, there had never been a sinless *person*, one who could completely *remove* sin and the barrier it had put between God and people. That is why He came to earth! He came to be the innocent substitute and pay our sins' penalty. There was no other way our relationship with God could be restored. There was no other way we could be forgiven!

Jesus lived a sinless life as a baby, a child, a teenager, and an adult. Read what 2 Corinthians 5:21 (page 884) says about Him.

What is your reaction to this verse?

Jesus knew what being the offering for our sin would entail for Him. On several occasions He foretold that He would be put to death and then be raised back to life. Let's look at a couple of these verses and note who He was talking to and what He told them.

Luke 18:31-33 (page 801)

Matthew 12:38-40 (page 743)

Mark 8:31-32a (page 769)

Did you notice that verse 32 said Jesus talked openly with them?

Jesus Is Tried and Condemned

However, as more people followed Jesus, the religious leaders became more outraged. They twisted His words, they tried to trick Him, and they threatened Him and the people who followed Him. They became so determined to silence Him that they were willing to do whatever it took regardless of how dishonest their actions were. They trumped up charges and had Him arrested. It's a chilling but riveting story.

Read Luke 22:54,63-71 and 23:1-25 (pages 805-806) and note the facts you find most interesting.

Isn't it interesting that when Pilate was face-to-face with Jesus, looking him squarely in the eye, one question was all he needed to ask Him to proclaim Him innocent? But Pilate had an angry crowd on his hands, and he needed to find a way out of the situation. Do you sense his relief in learning that Jesus was from Galilee, so he could pass Him off to Herod (verses 6-7)?

I think the picture that comes to light in verses 8-12 is the most fascinating. First you see Herod's excitement at getting to meet Jesus, because he's heard so much about Him. In fact, Herod's hoping to see Jesus perform a miracle. He immediately starts pelting Jesus with questions, but Jesus refuses to answer. Why do you think Jesus answered Pilate's one question but none of Herod's? Could there have been a difference in attitude between the two men? We don't know, but the next few verses give us a glimpse into the kind of man Herod was.

Rulers usually remain aloof from the behavior of the crowd, but Herod *joined* his soldiers in ridiculing Jesus (verse 11) even though, like Pilate, he didn't find him guilty. Most interesting of all to me is that Pilate and Herod, who'd been enemies up to that point, suddenly became friends as a result of their personal encounter with Jesus. Don't you wonder why?

Both leaders agreed Jesus was innocent. Both leaders were cowardly and yielded to mob mentality, condemning an innocent man to death. It was a terrible weight to carry, and perhaps it was this shared guilt that formed the unique bond of friendship.

What are your thoughts about this?

Even though Jesus was arrested, even though He was questioned, tortured, and questioned some more, even though He was tried by the legal system of the day, no one could find a legitimate reason for His arrest and conviction. And still He was sentenced to death! Why? Read Mark 14:61-64 (page 776).

Of course, that was the truth. Jesus *is* the Messiah. He *is* the Son of God. But the authorities proclaimed that the truth was a lie, and thus they condemned to death *the very one who had created them*, the *"author of life"* (Acts 3:15, page 832). Through the whole ordeal, Jesus never once defended Himself because the outcome of this outrageous injustice was the very reason He'd come to earth—to become our substitute, pay our sins' penalty for all time, and bring us back to God.

His betrayal, the illegal trials, whipping, and actual crucifixion were no surprise to Jesus. He knew the extreme suffering He would have to endure. This had all been prophesied many years earlier. Read about it in Isaiah 53:3-6 (page 559).

Now let's read Mark's account of these events in Mark 14:43–15:15 (pages 776-777). What do you find is different in Mark's account than Luke's?

We Are Restored to God

Jesus came to be our substitute and pay our sins' penalty. He willingly took our punishment in order to restore our relationship with God, so we could share in God's life now and forever. This is eternal life! *"We are made right with God by placing our faith in Jesus Christ.*

And this is true for everyone who believes, no matter who we are" (Romans 3:22, page 859).

Through His death and resurrection, Jesus conquered death forever. Read Romans 5:17 (page 860). His death and resurrection also overpowered Satan. And our relationship with Jesus has set us free from Satan's power. Read Hebrews 2:14-15 (page 921).

Jesus was not only our substitute and sacrifice. He also did the work of a priest in offering the sacrifice of Himself. *"It was necessary for him to be made in every respect like us, his brothers and sisters, so that he could be our merciful and faithful High Priest before God. Then he could offer a sacrifice that would take away the sins of the people"* (Hebrews 2:17). Isn't He amazing?

What in particular did Satan use to enslave us?

Never again do we need to fear death…because of what Jesus has done.

A Full and Rich Life Through Jesus

All the wonderful things Jesus has done for us have not changed the fact that we have free will. We can use it to our detriment, or we can use it to live the transformed life Jesus has given to us (Romans 12:1-2, page 866). This brings us to a final thought about why Jesus came to earth. Read John 10:10 (page 819).

What does a full, "*rich and satisfying life*" mean to you?

Other Bible translations of this verse say *"have life, and have it abundantly"* (NASB) or *"more and better life than they ever dreamed of"* (MSG). It sounds wonderful, doesn't it? It also sounds like something we've talked about previously in our study. Read 1 John 5:11-12 (page 943).

How do you compare the *"rich and satisfying life"* in John 10:10 and the *"life…in His Son"* that the apostle John describes in 1 John 5:11?

Consider the term *eternal life*. How do you think it is related to the *"rich and satisfying life"* and the *"life…in His Son"* mentioned above?

Too often we think of eternal life as something that starts when we die physically. But you could also call it "undying life" or "life that does not perish" (John 3:16, page 811). Read John 11:25-26 (page 820).

Is what Jesus says in verse 26 something that happens now, or after we die physically?

Yes! As we read earlier, *"Whoever has the Son has life"* (1 John 5:12, page 943). It's now! Let's look at one more verse that expresses this wonderful truth. Read 1 John 5:20 (page 944).

What is the progression? Complete the thoughts:

We know...

he has given...

so that...

And now...

because we...

He is...

and he is...

Did you catch that last phrase? Jesus Christ Himself is eternal life! If we have Christ in us, then we have eternal life—the *"rich and satisfying life"*—right now.

Read the following verses for a few more small samplings of the *"rich and satisfying life"* Jesus came to give us:

Romans 15:13 (page 868)

Philippians 4:7 (page 901)

Ephesians 1:4-5 (page 895)

Which verse spoke the most strongly to you?

So what did Jesus come to do? He came to cover it all: He came to pay for our sin and bring us back to God, and He came to give us life: a rich and satisfying life that never dies, now or ever. Past, present, and future—Jesus addressed it all because He loves us and wants to have a transforming relationship with us.

—————— *Personal Reflection and Application* ——————

From this chapter,

I see...

I believe...

I will...

Prayer

Thank you, Father, that Christ, who never sinned, became the offering for my sin, so that I could be made right with you through Him (2 Corinthians 5:21, page 884).

Thoughts, Notes, and Prayer Requests

5

What Is Jesus Doing Today?

On a trip to Israel, I visited the tomb where it's believed Jesus was buried. Tucked away in a quiet garden, it feels a hundred miles removed from the cacophony of the city just outside its gate. Gnarled, three- and four-thousand-year-old olive trees provide shade from the desert heat—the very same trees that once provided shade for Jesus.

Walking deeper into the garden, I caught sight of a rock outcropping into which a tomb had been carved. Even from a distance, a long jagged crack could be seen running the length of it—evidence, very possibly, of the earthquake that shook the area at the exact moment of Jesus' resurrection. The stone that once rolled over the tomb's opening is no longer there, but the groove, or trough, in which it rolled is.

I took my time approaching the tomb, pausing when I reached the doorway, overcome with emotion. *This was where my destiny had been settled!*

Taking a deep breath, I stooped down to enter through the low opening to the small, two-chambered tomb. Inside, I brushed my hand across the cool stone, choking back another wave of emotion before turning to leave.

The words carved over the inside of the opening took my breath away: "He is not here—He is risen."

Riveting words…the most wondrous words ever written! Words that changed history forever—changed *everything* forever! Words that proved Jesus spoke truth. He is indeed our Savior, our Rescuer—God in human form, who loved His creation so much that He endured the unendurable to have relationship with us.

Prayer

God, truly this is love, not that I loved you, but that you loved me and sent your Son as a sacrifice to take away my sin. Help me to experience this reality as the center of my life (1 John 4:10, page 943).

The Events of Jesus' Resurrection

As you would think, all four Gospels recount the incredible events surrounding Jesus' resurrection. Read Matthew 28:1-7 (page 760). Share the details you find most fascinating.

Let's put ourselves in this story to experience it more fully. Imagine the quiet of the early morning as the two grief-filled women walk toward the last place on earth they want to be walking—the tomb that holds the body of the beloved man who'd changed their lives. The man they thought was the Messiah, God's Chosen One—the man who'd filled their lives with purpose, who had *loved* them!

Now everything was in shambles. The man who they'd hoped would rescue Israel from Roman occupation was dead. Their friend was dead. *What would happen to them now? What could they hope for, who could they believe in now?* Can you hear their sorrowful murmurs or feel their despair?

Before they reach the tomb, there is a terrifying rumbling that causes the earth to tremble beneath their feet. They gasp and grab each other for support. *What on earth is happening?* They look toward the tomb but can't make sense of what they see. The guards, charged with making sure no one stole Jesus' body, are crumpled on the ground as if dead. The massive stone that should have been covering the tomb's opening is rolled back and—*are their eyes deceiving them?*—an *angel* is sitting on the stone! They've never seen an angel before, but that's what he has to be. His face is shining so brightly it is like looking at a flash of lightning.

If you had been there with the women, how would you have processed the scene before you?

What would you have thought when the angel showed you the empty tomb?

Did you sense the urgency in the angel's words as he informed the women of their most exclusive assignment?

What do you suppose it was like? Do you think their minds were still reeling? Or did they realize the honor God had just bestowed on them—to proclaim the most wonderful news ever proclaimed throughout all of history? *Jesus is not dead*—He is risen (verse 7)!

Now read Matthew 28:8 (page 760). Can you imagine their chaotic emotion as they rush from the garden, hearts pounding? Not only are they still shaking with fear from the last few moments, but intense joy is now pulsing through them. *Everything Jesus told them has happened!* He did not stay dead. Best of all, the angel had just said they would see Him very shortly.

I doubt their hearts had yet returned to a normal pace when the next amazing thing happens. Read verses 9 and 10. Put yourself in place of the women. What do you feel when you read these two verses?

What significance can be drawn from Jesus appearing first to the women?

Not everyone was experiencing the same joyous disbelief. Some, in fact, were experiencing a terrified disbelief. Read Matthew 27:62-65 and then Matthew 28:11-15 (page 760) to see how Jesus' enemies dealt with these events.

What was the plan they came up with?

If you read further in the Bible and also consult other sources from that time, you will find out that Jesus' enemies never denied that His body had disappeared and couldn't be found. The evidence was too strong, too complete. The best they could do was to concoct a story.

It is never pleasant to be on the losing team, is it? And for *this* team, losing was a matter of life and death. Imagine the sickening realization they each had to struggle with as they were forced to live with the worst choice of their lives.

And now, some 2000 years later, the same choice is in front of you. Are you for Jesus or against Him? Are you on the side of the two Marys…or on the side of the leading priests and elders, who denied that God had anything to do with Jesus' release from the tomb? There's no in-between. You are either with Jesus or against Him. Where do you stand?

After the Resurrection

For those who followed Jesus, the 40 days following His resurrection were an amazing time as they walked and talked with the man whose execution some of them had seen with their own eyes. And yet, just as He'd promised, He was no longer dead. Read Luke's description of that time in Acts 1:1-11 (page 830).

What does it tell you?

As thrilled as His disciples were to see Him again, you can imagine how difficult it was for them to truly believe what they were seeing and hearing. Jesus understood this and addressed their doubts.

Turn to Luke 24:35-49 (page 808). How did He address their doubt?

What do you learn about a glorified body from this passage?

If we have Christ's life in us, the Bible says that we too will one day have glorified bodies (Philippians 3:20-21, page 901)! Just as we now have spiritual life that will never die, we must also have bodies to match (1 Corinthians 15:50,53, page 880). It's exhilarating to think about, isn't it?

During the days following His resurrection, Jesus appeared to many people. Read the following Bible passages and note to whom He appeared:

John 20:14-18 (page 828)

Luke 24:13-15 (page 807)

John 20:26-29 (page 828)

John 21:1 (page 829)

1 Corinthians 15:5 (page 879)

1 Corinthians 15:6 (page 879)

1 Corinthians 15:7 (page 879)

At the end of the 40 days there was another remarkable occurrence. Read about it in Luke 24:50-53 (page 808). What does it say happened?

God is *omnipresent*—He is present everywhere. Where do the following verses say Jesus is now?

Colossians 3:1 (page 903)

Hebrews 12:2 (page 927)

Galatians 2:20 (page 891)

Ephesians 3:16-19 (page 896)

Jesus Is Our Advocate, the One Who Intercedes for Us

It's encouraging to know that Jesus is present with God in heaven *and* lives within each of us who have welcomed Him into our hearts as Lord and Savior. But that's not all. There is still another action that Christ is taking now on our behalf—yes, right now. Read the following passages and summarize what they say.

Hebrews 7:24-25 (pages 923-924)

Romans 8:31-34 (page 863)

1 John 2:1 (page 941)

Jesus intercedes on our behalf because of His never-ending desire and commitment to have a relationship with you and me. This means He will never give up on us. Read Romans 8:35-39 (page 863).

The word *intercede* comes from a Latin word that literally translates "to go between." Webster defines *intercede* as "to intervene between parties with a view to reconciling differences." Jesus is truly our "go-between" with God!

Make a list of everything this passage tells you about the benefits of being chosen and loved by Jesus.

Look over your list. Do you see what incredible lengths Jesus goes to in His love for us? And nothing can interrupt that love—no power in the universe can separate us from His love. How wonderful it is to know that!

Another Advocate

When we receive Christ, He makes His home inside us. Read John 14:16-20 (page 823) and Romans 8:9-11 (page 862).

Who else besides Christ do these passages mention?

What is this other Person called in John 14:16-20?

When we receive salvation through believing in Christ's death and resurrection, He lives in us through the presence of His Holy Spirit.

The Spirit is always with us to teach us and guide us and to remind us that we belong to God.

⬤⬤⬤⬤⬤⬤⬤⬤⬤⬤⬤⬤⬤⬤

Let's take a few moments to go back over the key parts of what we've been learning about Jesus.

What did the death of Jesus accomplish for us? Write your answer after each verse.

The study *Who Is the Holy Spirit?* can make a wonderful follow-up to *Who Is Jesus?* For more information, see "Stonecroft Resources" in the back of this book.

Romans 5:8-9 (page 860)

Romans 5:10 (page 860)

The last part of this verse reinforces a wonderful truth that we have seen throughout this study! After we have invited Jesus into our lives as our Savior and Lord, we are not the same. His resurrection life is now our life, and the Holy Spirit lives and works in us. That is why it is necessary for us to live consistently with who we now are. This is everything in the Christian life. We cannot live it by ourselves.

It is not an independent life. Only because we are now connected with God through the Holy Spirit in us can we have and live the kind of life He wants for us.

However, having God's Spirit in us does not mean we suddenly start living a perfect and sin-free existence. There will be times when we make wrong choices. In other words, we will still sin.

To confess. The New Testament was written in Greek, and the word translated into English as *confess* could be literally translated "to say the same thing." In other words, confession is simply agreeing with God in regard to what He says about sin.

What does 1 John 1:8-9 (page 941) tell us to do about this?

What is the assurance we have?

We can be utterly confident that God the Father will always welcome us! Here's another wonderful assurance that John the apostle gives us: *"If anyone does sin, we have an advocate who pleads our case before the Father. He is Jesus Christ, the one who is truly righteous"* (1 John 2:1, page 941).

─────── *Personal Reflection and Application* ───────

From this chapter,

I see…

I believe…

I will…

─────────────── ❧ ───────────────

Prayer:

God, thank you for your incredible love for me. Thank you that I can now love in your way because you have loved me. Please help me to love you with all of my heart, soul, mind, and strength. And as I do that, help me to love others just as I love myself (1 John 4:19, page 943, and Mark 12:30-31, page 773).

─────── *Thoughts, Notes, and Prayer Requests* ───────

6

How Does Jesus' Life Make
a Difference in My Life?

One of my most vivid childhood memories is standing beside my grandmother on a Sunday morning in the tiny country church she attended. Everyone was singing one of those old hymns that has almost passed into oblivion now. I remember looking up at her and seeing the most joyous smile on her face—she almost glowed.

The song was "When We See Christ." It spoke of how life's difficulties would seem tiny in comparison to seeing Jesus. Seeing Him would make everything worth it. His loving face would wipe out the memory of all the sadness and struggle. And the final words encouraged us to keep going courageously till we were with Christ.

Many years before, my grandmother had been widowed on Christmas Day in the middle of the Depression. She had seven small children to feed and a crushing farm debt she didn't know how she would pay. She also had a transformational relationship with God that kept these staggering challenges in perspective. She knew that her Savior, Jesus, had said, *"Humanly speaking, it is impossible. But with God everything is possible"* (Matthew 19:26, page 750). Even more important than that, she knew that one day she would indeed see Jesus, and that would make everything she was experiencing on earth absolutely worth it.

Prayer

God, thank you for your Son's promise to one day come for me, so that I can always be where He is. Thank you that where He is, you are. Open my heart to what you want me to understand about Jesus' return (John 14:2-3, page 823).

God's Plan

In chapter 4, we learned that God has always wanted a close relationship with us, His creation. Before time began, He knew He would create people. He knew He would give them the freedom to choose whether they would obey Him or not. He also knew people would misuse this freedom and choose to sin rather than stay intimately connected with Him.

Knowing all this, before He even created us, God devised a plan by which we could be forgiven and be restored to a close relationship with Him. The plan was that He would send His Son to be born of a virgin—born as a human being—here on earth. Jesus would show us who the Father was and how much He wanted us back. He would live a sinless life and then He, who was perfect, would pay for the sins of imperfect people.

Although Jesus was completely innocent of all charges brought against Him, He was nevertheless sentenced to death by crucifixion—a terrible way to die. Because of our sin and His love for us, He willingly suffered an excruciating death. He was buried, just like all who die—but on the third day He rose from the dead. For the next 40 days following His resurrection He was seen by many people, talking to them, touching them, and even eating with them. Though He was going to leave, because He loves us He made a plan to give us the Holy Spirit—our Helper and Advocate—to be with us. Finally He ascended into heaven.

God the Father did all of this because He loves us and wants to be in relationship with us now and forever. And the result of His love is that our debt of sin was paid in full. God offers forgiveness, salvation, and the gift of eternal life, which are provided only through Christ's life, death, and resurrection.

Jesus Is Going to Return

You might be wondering what it will be like to live forever with Christ. The concept and complexity of eternity can bring questions, even fears to mind. And His disciples shared some of the same worries and concerns we experience today.

Assurance from Jesus

Jesus understands our limitations, and He addresses how He is preparing a place for us to live with Him. Read John 14:1-4 (page 823).

Speaking of our future home in the Father's house, how do Christ's words to not worry and trust God speak to you personally?

Do you find any exceptions in Jesus' promise in verse 3—any reason He might not follow through on what He says?

Jesus tells us to *"trust in God, and trust also in me."* Remember, God keeps His promises! The words and heart of Christ are clear as He speaks of the vast amount of room available to those who trust in Him. Again, His desire is that all would come into relationship with Him—that none would die without Him.

The Judgment to Come

Whether we have placed our trust in Christ or not, the Bible teaches that we all will see Him one day. Read Revelation 1:7 (page 949).

Everyone! That includes those who want to see Him and those who don't; those who believe He is God and those who believe He is just a historical figure— or those who don't believe at all. Everyone will one day see Jesus, and on that day He will be recognized by all as God's Chosen One!

Throughout the New Testament, the emphasis is not so much on *where* we will be after our bodies die, but *with whom* we will be. Read another example of this in Paul's words in 2 Corinthians 5:6-8 (page 884).

Although many people don't believe that Jesus is God, when He returns *everyone* will suddenly know and believe. The Bible also tells us that everyone will see Him exalted and honored and will bow before Him. Read Philippians 2:10-11 (page 900).

What will everyone say?

The Bible has much to say about those who have not accepted God's forgiveness. Without the Son they do not have life (1 John 5:11-12, page 943). Read Revelation 20:14b-15 (page 961).

When people talk about being saved, they are talking about being rescued from separation from God that lasts forever and from punishment that lasts forever. We must remember that *it is absolutely not God's desire for anyone to perish forever.* He has made it possible for everyone to be rescued. What do the following passages say?

1 Timothy 2:3-4 (page 910)

2 Peter 3:9 (page 939)

John 3:16 (page 811)

Now read Acts 17:31 (page 846) and 2 Thessalonians 1:7-9 (page 908). When we read what God says about His righteous judgment, we realize that our acceptance of Jesus will save us from eternal destruction and being forever separated from the Lord.

What is your reaction to this?

If we have received Christ, the judgment we undergo will have nothing to do with whether we have a relationship with God. Through Jesus, it is an accomplished fact that we are God's children. Instead, we will be judged regarding the things we have done. Read 2 Corinthians 5:9-10 (page 884).

What do these verses say about the judgment of Christians?

How will this affect the way you spend your time?

A Wonderful Future

For those who are His children, God is preparing something wonderful beyond imagining. How do the following verses describe it?

1 John 3:2-3 (page 942)

Revelation 21:3-5 (page 961)

Revelation 22:3-5 (page 962)

It sounds fantastic, doesn't it?
Which description did you like best, and why?

The Choice

From what we have learned in this chapter, we know there is a choice to make. According to John 3:36 (page 811), what is it?

Nothing of our own—our intelligence, our religion, or our good works—gives us entrance into heaven. We may know about the Bible; we may even live a moral life and do many good things. But we can't enter heaven without God's life—life that we receive by believing in His Son. We can spend forever with God only when we make the decision to believe that Jesus is who He said He was.

We don't have to do anything before making this decision. We don't have to clean up our lives or try to be a better person first. We can just come to Jesus as we are. Read the following two promises of Jesus. What do they say?

John 6:37 (page 814)

Matthew 11:28-29 (page 742)

What remarkable, hope-filled words! What do these verses say to you?

If you've never made the choice to believe in and receive Christ Jesus as your Savior, it is very easy to do.

First, recognize that God created you to be in fellowship with Him. He loves you and wants to fill you with His love so you can love Him with all of your being.

Acknowledge that you are a sinner, separated from God, and that Jesus died on the cross to pay the death penalty for your sin and bring you back to God. The fact that Jesus rose from the dead and is alive today is what makes a relationship with Him possible.

Would you like to have such a relationship? That can happen right now if you like. All you have to do is talk to Jesus as if He were sitting right beside you. Tell Him that you agree with Him about your sins— the sins that cost Him His life. Let Him know that you are ready to give your life to Him and allow Him to live in you. Ask Him to come into your life and forgive your sins.

When you say these things to Jesus, your relationship with Him begins. You are transformed into a brand-new person, complete and without sin in God's eyes. (See 2 Corinthians 5:17, page 884, and Colossians 1:21-22, page 902.) This is a decision you will never regret.

As you begin to talk with God every day and read your Bible, as you allow yourself to be guided by the Holy Spirit, God will become more and more real to you.

It is very important that you tell someone about the decision you've made. Don't keep it a secret, because you want your faith to start growing immediately, and other Christians can help you with this.

Long before I was born, my grandmother made this very same decision. It's why that song she sang filled her with such joy. She knew she would one day see Jesus as He is, and it filled her with anticipation.

And now we know that one day every person—living and dead— will also see Him. If you've surrendered your life to Him, this is a day to anticipate with all of your heart! Jesus, our beloved Savior, is returning. When He does, you will at last see for yourself the wonderful and eternal home He has prepared for you—*and it will all be worth it!*

───────── *Personal Reflection and Application* ─────────

From this chapter,

I see...

I believe...

I will...

─────────────── ∞ ───────────────

Prayer

Dear God, your unfailing love for me is better than life itself; how I praise you! I will praise you as long as I live, lifting up my hands to you in prayer. You satisfy me more than the richest feast. I will praise you with songs of joy. Thank you for what I have learned about your Son, Jesus, through this study (Psalm 63:3-5, page 441).

─────── *Thoughts, Notes, and Prayer Requests* ───────

_____

_____

_____

_____

_____

Journal Pages

Know God

It does not matter what has happened in your past. No matter what you've done, no matter how you've lived your life,

God is personally interested in you right now.
He cares about you.

God understands your frustration, your loneliness, your heart-aches. He wants each of us to come to Him, to know Him personally.

God is so rich in mercy, and he loved us so much, that even
though we were dead because of our sins, he gave us
life when he raised Christ from the dead.
(It is only by God's grace that you have been saved!)

—*Ephesians 2:4-5 (page 895)*

God loves you.

He created you in His image. His desire is to be in relationship with you. He wants you to belong to Him.

Sadly, our sin gets in the way. It separates us from God, and without Him we are dead in our spirits. There is nothing we can do to close that gap. There is nothing we can do to give ourselves life. No matter how well we may behave.

But God loves us so much He made a way to eliminate that gap and give us new life, His kind of life—to restore the relationship. His love for you is so great, so tremendous, that He sent Jesus Christ, His only Son, to earth to live, and then die—filling the gap and taking the punishment we deserve for refusing God's ways.

> God made Christ, who never sinned,
> to be the offering for our sin, so that we could
> be made right with God through Christ.
>
> —*2 Corinthians 5:21 (page 884)*

Jesus Christ, God's Son, not only died to pay the penalty for your sin, but He conquered death when He rose from the grave. He is ready to share His life with you.

**Christ reconciles us to God. Jesus is alive today.
He will give you a new beginning and a newly created life
when you surrender control of your life to Him.**

> Anyone who belongs to Christ has become a new
> person. The old life is gone; a new life has begun!
>
> —*2 Corinthians 5:17 (page 884)*

How do you begin this new life? You need to realize

> …the necessity of repenting from sin and turning to
> God, and of having faith in our Lord Jesus.
>
> —*Acts 20:21 (page 849)*

Agree with God about your sins and believe that Jesus came to save you, that He is your Savior and Lord. Ask Him to lead your life.

God loved the world so much that he gave his
one and only Son, so that everyone who believes in him
will not perish but have eternal life.
God sent his Son into the world not to judge the
world, but to save the world through him.

—*John 3:16-17 (page 811)*

Pray something like this:

Jesus, I do believe you are the Son of God and that you died on the cross to pay the penalty for my sin. Forgive me. I turn away from sin and choose to live a life that pleases you. Enter my life as my Savior and Lord.

I want to follow you and make you the leader of my life.

Thank you for your gift of eternal life and for the Holy Spirit, who has now come to live in me. I ask this in your name. Amen.

God puts His Spirit inside you, who enables you to live a life pleasing to Him. He gives you new life that will never die, that will last forever—eternally.

When you surrender your life to Jesus Christ, you are making the most important decision of your life. Stonecroft would like to offer you a free download of *A New Beginning*, a short Bible study that will help you as you begin your new life in Christ. Go to **stonecroft.org/newbeginning**.

If you'd like to talk with someone right now about this prayer, call **1.888.NEED.HIM**.

Who Is Stonecroft?

Every day Stonecroft communicates the Gospel in meaningful ways. Whether through a speaker sharing her transformational story, or side by side in a ministry service project, the Gospel of Jesus Christ goes forward. In one-on-one conversations with a long-term friend, and through well-developed online and print resources, the Gospel of Jesus Christ goes forward.

For nearly 75 years, we've been introducing women to Jesus Christ and training them to share His Good News with others.

Stonecroft understands and appreciates the influence of one woman's life. When you reach her, you touch everyone she knows—her family, friends, neighbors, and co-workers. The real Truth of the Gospel brings real redemption into real lives.

Our life-changing, faith-building community resources include:

- *STONECROFT BIBLE AND BOOK STUDIES*—both topical and traditional chapter-by-chapter studies. Stonecroft studies are designed for those in small groups—those who know Christ and those who do not yet know Him—to simply yet profoundly discover God's Word together.

- *OUTREACH EVENTS AND SERVICE ACTIVITIES*—set the stage for women to be encouraged and equipped to hear and share the Gospel with their communities. Whether in a large venue, workshop, or small group setting, women are prepared to serve their communities with the love of Christ.

- *SMALL-GROUP STUDIES FOR CHRISTIANS*—these studies engage believers in God's heart for those who do not know Him. Our most recent, the Aware series, includes *Aware, Belong*, and *Call*.

- *STONECROFT LIFE PUBLICATIONS*—clearly explain the Gospel through stories of people whose lives have been transformed by Jesus Christ.

- *STONECROFT PRAYER*—foundational for everything we do, prayer groups, materials, and training set the focus on our reliance on God for all ministry and to share the Gospel.

- *STONECROFT'S WEBSITE*—stonecroft.org—offering fresh content daily to equip and encourage you.

Dedicated and enthusiastic Stonecroft staff serve you via Divisional Field Directors stationed across the United States, and a Home Office team overseeing the leadership of tens of thousands of dedicated volunteers worldwide.

Visit **stonecroft.org** to learn more about these and other outstanding Stonecroft resources, groups, and events.

Contact us via **connections@stonecroft.org** or **800.525.8627**.

Stonecroft

Books for Further Study

Bruce, F.F. *The New Testament Documents: Are They Reliable?* Grand Rapids, MI: Wm. B. Eerdmans Publishing Co., 2003.

Lockyer, Herbert. *All the Divine Names and Titles in the Bible*. Grand Rapids, MI: Zondervan Publishing House, 1988.

_____. *All the Parables of the Bible*. Grand Rapids, MI: Zondervan Publishing House, 1988.

Lotz, Anne Graham. *Just Give Me Jesus*. Nashville, TN: Word Publishing, 2000.

McDowell, Josh. *The New Evidence That Demands a Verdict*. Nashville, TN: Thomas Nelson, Inc., 1999.

Pentecost, J. Dwight. *The Words and Works of Jesus Christ*. Grand Rapids, MI: Zondervan Publishing House, 1981.

Purnell, Dick. *Knowing God by His Names*. Eugene, OR: Harvest House Publishers, 2005.

Strobel, Lee. *The Case for Christ*. Grand Rapids, MI: Zondervan Publishing House, 1998.

Yancey, Philip. *The Jesus I Never Knew.* Grand Rapids, MI: Zondervan Publishing House, 2002.

Stonecroft Resources

Stonecroft Bible Studies make the Word of God accessible to everyone. These studies allow small groups to discover the adventure of a personal relationship with God and introduce others to God's unlimited love, grace, forgiveness, and power. To learn more, visit **stonecroft.org/biblestudies.**

Who Is Jesus? (6 chapters)
He was a rebel against the status quo. The religious community viewed Him as a threat. The helpless and outcast considered Him a friend. Explore the life and teachings of Jesus—this rebel with a cause who challenges us today to a life of radical faith.

What Is God Like? (6 chapters)
What is God like? Is He just a higher power? Has He created us and left us on our own? Where is He when things don't make sense? Discover what the Bible tells us about God and how we can know Him in a life-transforming way.

Who Is the Holy Spirit? (6 chapters)
Are you living up to the full life that God wants for you? Learn about the Holy Spirit, our Helper and power source for everyday living, who works in perfect harmony with God the Father and Jesus the Son.

Connecting with God (8 chapters)
Prayer is our heart-to-heart communication with our heavenly Father. This study examines the purpose, power, and elements of prayer, sharing biblical principles for effective prayer.

Prayer Worth Repeating (15 devotions)

There is no place where your prayers to the one and only God cannot penetrate, no circumstance prayers cannot impact. As the mother of adult children, your greatest influence into their lives is through prayer. *Prayer Worth Repeating* is a devotional prayer guide designed to focus your prayers and encourage you to trust God more deeply as He works in the lives of your adult children.

Pray & Play Devotional (12 devotions)

It's playgroup with a purpose! Plus Mom tips. For details on starting a Pray & Play group, visit **stonecroft.org/prayandplay** or call **800.525.8627.**

Aware (5 lessons)

Making Jesus known every day starts when we are *Aware* of those around us. This dynamic Stonecroft Small Group Bible Study about "Always Watching and Responding with Encouragement" equips and engages people in the initial steps to the joys of evangelism.

Belong (6 lessons)

For many in today's culture, the desire to belong is often part of their journey to believe. *Belong* explores how we can follow in Jesus' footsteps—and walk with others on their journey to belong.

Call (7 lessons)

Every day we meet people without Christ. That is God's intention.

He wants His people to initiate and build friendships. He wants us together. *Call* helps us take a closer look at how God makes Himself known through our relationships with those around us.

Discover together God's clear calling for you and those near to you.

Order these and other Stonecroft Resources at our online store at **stonecroft.org/store.**

If you have been encouraged and brought closer to God by this study, please consider giving a gift to Stonecroft so that others can experience life change as well. You can find information about giving online at **stonecroft.org.** (Click on the "Donate" tab.)

If you'd like to give via telephone, please contact us at **800.525.8627**. Or you can mail your gift to

Stonecroft
10561 Barkley, Suite 500
Overland Park, KS 66212

Stonecroft

10561 Barkley, Suite 500
Overland Park, KS 66212
Telephone: 800.525.8627
E-mail: connections@stonecroft.org

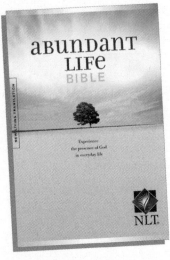

Abundant Life Bible
New Living Translation
Holy Bible

*Experience the presence of God
in everyday life*

Stonecroft is pleased to partner with Tyndale to offer the New Living Translation Holy Bible as the companion for our newly released Stonecroft Bible Studies.

The New Living Translation translators set out to render the message of the original Scripture language texts into clear, contemporary English. In this *translation*, scholars kept the concerns of both formal-equivalence and dynamic-equivalence in mind. Their goal was a Bible that is faithful to the ancient texts and eminently readable. The result is a translation that is both accurate and powerful.

TRUTH MADE CLEAR

Features of the Abundant Life Bible

- Features are easy-to-use and written for people who don't yet know Jesus Christ personally.
- Unequaled clarity and accuracy
- Dictionary included
- Concordance included
- Old Testament included

- Introductory notes on important abundant life topics such as:

Gospel presentation	Practical guidance
Joy	Life's tough issues
Peace	Prayer

- Insights from a relationship with Jesus Christ.
- Ideal Scripture text for those not familiar with the Bible!

 Tyndale House Publishers

To order: stonecroft.org/store
888.819.5218